THE CHINA CLIPPER

by
Peter Guttmacher

Crestwood House
New York

Maxwell Macmillan Canada
Toronto

Maxwell Macmillan International
New York   Oxford   Singapore   Sydney

Library of Congress Cataloging-in-Publication Data
Guttmacher, Peter

    The China Clipper / by Peter Guttmacher. — 1st ed.
      p.   cm. — (Those Daring Machines)
    Includes index.
    Summary: Traces the development of the China Clipper, the 26-ton flying cruise ship that pioneered aviation from the United States to Asia, in the 1930s.
    ISBN 0-89686-826-5   0-382-24752-3 (pbk.)
    1. China Clipper (Airplane) — History — Juvenile literature. 2. Pan American World Airways, Inc. — History — Juvenile literature. 3. Transpacific flights — History — Juvenile literature. [1. China Clipper (Airplane) 2. Pan American World Airways, Inc. 3. Transpacific flights.] I. Title. II. Series.
TL684.G84 1994
387.7'09164 — dc20   93 - 46204

Copyright ® 1994 Crestwood House, Macmillan Publishing Company

All rights reserved. No part of this book may be reproduced or transmitted in any form or by any means, electronic or mechanical, including photocopying, recording, or by any information storage and retrieval system, without permission in writing from the Publisher.

Crestwood House
Macmillan Publishing Company
866 Third Avenue
New York, NY 10022

Maxwell Macmillan Canada, Inc.
1200 Eglinton Avenue East
Suite 200
Don Mills, Ontario M3C 3N1

Macmillan Publishing Company is part of the Maxwell Communication Group of Companies

First Edition

Printed in the United States of America

10 9 8 7 6 5 4 3 2 1

Created and developed by The Learning Source

Acknowledgments

We would like to thank the many people who helped make this book possible. Our special thanks go to Jeff Kreindler and the Pan Am Historical Association, whose help in locating and obtaining photos was invaluable.

Photo Credits
All photos in this book courtesy of the Pan Am Historical Society/Archives and Special Collections Department, Otto G. Richter Library, University of Miami, Coral Gables, Florida.

CONTENTS

Chapter 1 Takeoff 5

Chapter 2 Juan Trippe's Seaplane 11

Chapter 3 The Flying Boats 17

Chapter 4 Island Bases 24

Chapter 5 "An Uneventful Trip" 28

Chapter 6 Flying to China 32

Chapter 7 The End of an Era 39

Glossary 46

Further Reading 47

Index 48

1

TAKEOFF

On November 22, 1935, crowds rushed to San Francisco Bay. People stood on tiptoe, jumped up on their cars, and scrambled onto rooftops for a better look. Overhead, fireworks rained down on the harbor where boats sounded their horns. A company of Boy Scouts unfurled the American flag. The air was charged with excitement.

At the center of this celebration, the main attraction floated calmly on the water. It was a huge airplane known as the *China Clipper*.

The *China Clipper* was no ordinary airplane. To begin with, it was a seaplane — a plane that landed and took off from water. This flying boat, as it was called, had a watertight body that let it float just like a ship.

The clipper was also enormous. From its rounded nose to its upswept tail fins, it measured 91 feet. Its height, from the base of its curved hull to the top of its wing, was 25 feet. From tip to tip, the wings spanned 130 feet. The

The *China Clipper*'s flights took it to far-off places that captured people's imaginations.

Crowds gathered to watch the *China Clipper* take off on November 22, 1935.

China Clipper was the biggest and most beautifully built airplane the world had yet seen.

Mounted in the wings were four 830-horsepower Pratt and Whitney engines. Each of them was as powerful as a locomotive. All that power wasn't for show, though. It would be needed to pull the 26-ton clipper out of the water.

Amid the hubbub, the engines roared to life and warmed up for takeoff. Hundreds of newsreel cameras focused on the plane. Reporters swarmed the docks. Around the world, millions of people tuned in their radios to hear history in the making.

This fantastic event was a shining moment in the dark depths of the **Great Depression**. For a short time, people could forget about such problems as hunger and unemployment. Perhaps for a moment the *China Clipper* could help even the poorest folks believe in magic.

Proud words of congratulations from President Franklin D. Roosevelt were aired to the world. Then came a voice radioed from Hawaii: "Pan American Airways ocean air base Number 1, Honolulu, Hawaii, standing by for orders." Similar messages soon came in from the Pacific islands of Midway, Wake, and Guam, as well as from Luzon, in the Philippines, on the other side of the Pacific Ocean.

Among the many people gathered that day in San Francisco, the proudest of all was a man named Juan Trippe. It was his vision and drive that had turned the dream of a **transpacific** route into reality. At 3:45 P.M. Trippe's message to the pilot, Captain Edwin Musick, boomed over the loudspeaker. "Cast off and depart for Manila in accordance therewith," Trippe's voice called out.

"Aye, aye, sir," came the reply from the clipper's pilot.

With that, the harbor crew unleashed the "silver-winged whale," as they called the plane. As the clipper taxied into takeoff position, a brass band struck up "The Star-Spangled

Banner." Then the craft shot forward, gaining speed to begin its skyward climb.

On board the clipper were 1,879 pounds of mail — more than a million letters. The mail had been delivered to the plane by stagecoach. Stagecoaches once had carried mail across the American frontier. Now, this special coach-to-plane delivery was set up to dramatize how much American transportation had changed in the 50 years since the time of the stagecoach.

An old stagecoach brought the mail — and some drama — to the *China Clipper*'s takeoff.

The *China Clipper* was a great leap forward for transportation. In fact, this plane was about to make the world a much smaller place. Four days after leaving San Francisco, the plane would arrive in Manila, the capital of the Philippines.

The flight would cover 8,210 miles. It would be the longest overwater crossing in history. No other plane in the world could span even just the first leg of the trip, from San Francisco to Honolulu.

In flight, the *China Clipper* soared 9,000 feet above the sea with the grace and beauty of a swan. But the clipper was more than a beautiful sight. It was a true engineering marvel. Fully loaded, it cruised at 150 miles per hour and could do 3,200 miles nonstop. Built into its bold design were backup systems that would let the *China Clipper* handle just about any kind of trouble imaginable. The plane was ready for anything from violent storms to most mechanical failures.

As it left, the clipper passed the unfinished Golden Gate Bridge.

While the outside of the clipper was the perfect blend of technology and adventure, the inside was the height of 1930s luxury and romance. Ready for passengers, the *China Clipper* was an inviting, softly lit space. A richly furnished sitting room could be turned into a formal dining room. At night, while on the way to far-off lands, passengers slept in curtained berths. No wonder people would say that flying in the *China Clipper* was like riding on a real-life magic carpet.

Not everyone, of course, was ready to believe in this new flying machine. In the 1930s, many people still refused to take air travel seriously. To them, flying was something for daredevils, adventurers, or movie stars. But changing people's minds was part of the clipper's job. Juan Trippe and the leaders of Pan American Airways hoped this amazing plane would show that air service was reliable, routine, and safe.

Still, there were no passengers on the *China Clipper*'s first run to Manila. Instead, the plane carried its crew and that huge cargo of mail. But as the days and months to come would show, it had the future of **commercial aviation** riding on its wings.

JUAN TRIPPE'S SEAPLANE

Juan Trippe was born into a wealthy New Jersey family in 1899. Despite his Spanish first name, Trippe was descended from British-American ancestors, many of them seagoing adventurers. One ancestor had fought against pirates and had been rewarded with a sword of valor by the British crown. Other relatives had sailed out of Baltimore Harbor in command of great **clipper ships**.

Trippe, too, dreamed of traveling to faraway places. But he wanted to go by air rather than by sea. As a teenager, he attended the Curtis Flying School and the Marconi Radio School. In 1917 he left Yale University and enlisted in the Navy Flying Corps. There he earned his wings, becoming a full-fledged pilot. When he returned to college, he organized the Yale Flying Club.

Although his parents did not approve, Trippe's hobby became his career. In 1922 he bought nine navy surplus seaplanes for $500 each. He turned his bargain fleet into Long Island Airways. The little airline carried the rich and famous on short flights to resorts like Atlantic City and the Long Island seashore. As the company's president, sales manager, chief pilot, and mechanic, Trippe learned every part of the aviation business.

In three years he was ready to expand. With some wealthy college pals, Trippe bought another small airline and merged with a third. The new company, Colonial Air Transport, flew mail from New York to Boston.

Trippe's ambitions grew. He wanted to circle the world by air, carrying passengers as well as mail and other cargo. Delivering airmail for the U.S. Post Office would pay the way. So Trippe sold his share of Colonial and organized the Aviation Corporation of America. This new company in turn bought a new airline that was just getting itself off the ground—Pan American Airways, or Pan Am, for short.

Pan Am had been granted a high-paying contract to fly the U.S. mail from Key West, Florida, to Havana, Cuba. There was one hitch, though. The first mail delivery to Cuba had to take place by October 19, 1927. Otherwise, the deal was off. But neglect had turned the runways in Key West into swamps, and there was no time to repair the airstrips. All was not lost, however. A seaplane could take off and land without a runway!

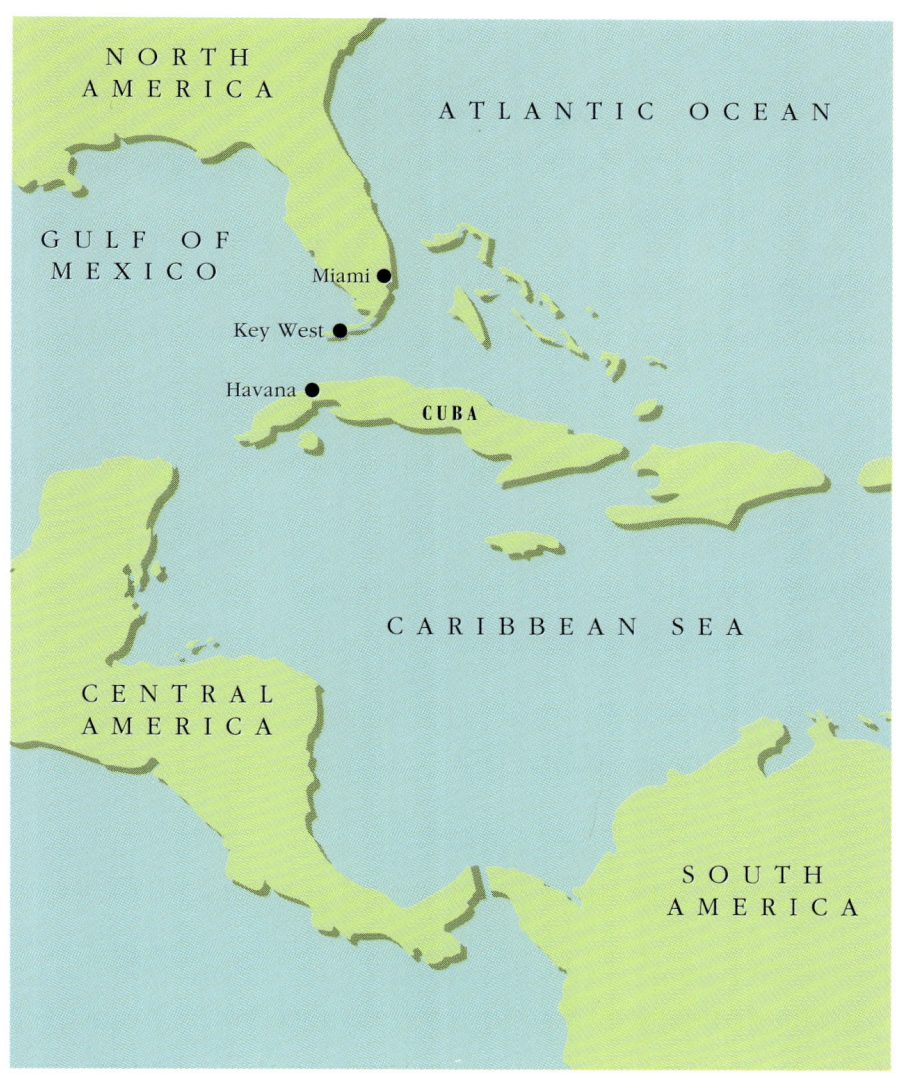

A flight from Key West to Havana was the first step in Juan Trippe's plan for his company.

On October 19, Trippe hired a seaplane and pilot to carry 30,000 letters across the 90-mile stretch of water from Key West to Havana. Pan Am had made the deadline — just barely! With that flight, Pan American Airways became an international carrier.

As Pan Am grew, so did Trippe's ambitions. He hired the best people in aviation to help make his dream come true. André Preister, a well-known engineer from Royal Dutch Airlines, joined Pan Am. Another new employee was Hugo Leuritz, an expert in navigation and communication. He set up Pan Am's radio lifeline for flights over water and unfamiliar ground. Edwin Musick, a former airplane daredevil and World War I flying ace, was also hired. Musick became Pan Am's chief pilot and flight instructor.

For Pan Am's technical adviser, Trippe chose Charles Lindbergh. In 1927 Lindbergh had made the first solo, nonstop flight across the Atlantic. His New York-to-Paris flight had made history, and the flier was now a world-famous hero. Lindbergh's name helped create the right reputation for Pan Am — adventurous, successful, and safe.

By 1930 Trippe had established a network of routes to Central America, South America, and the Caribbean. Pan Am flight crews braved dreadful tropical storms. The crews navigated their way to remote runways carved from thick jungle. Amazingly, however, Trippe's global plans made the South American routes look easy. He was gearing up for transatlantic flights to England — the hub of European travel. Air routes to London would be a gold mine.

But again there was a problem. Finding sites for planes to land and refuel was tricky. The United States controlled little land along the Atlantic route. England and France were the landlords from Bermuda to Newfoundland. Neither country would agree to give Pan Am landing rights before it had its own planes in service. But Trippe was ready and saw no reason to wait.

In May 1934, Trippe met with the Pan Am board of directors. The board members expected him to discuss plans for the Atlantic

Flights across the Atlantic were difficult — in more ways than one.

route to Europe. Instead, he shocked them with a completely different announcement: "Gentlemen," he declared, "we are about to fly the Pacific."

It was a startling decision. And to accomplish Trippe's goal, his old friend the seaplane would have to make a spectacular comeback.

THE FLYING BOATS

The long-distance transpacific route was going to be expensive. Pan Am needed a plane that could tackle more than 8,000 miles. The first hop, from San Francisco to Pearl Harbor—just outside Honolulu, Hawaii—was more than 2,400 miles nonstop. Some of the other stops would have no airstrips at all. So the airliner would have to be a seaplane.

The plane also had to carry enough payload—things it was paid to transport—to make a profit. So, in addition to cargo, Trippe wanted to carry passengers. Here, he had to compete with ocean liners, which offered comfort, luxury, and romance. Moreover, cruise ships had won public trust.

In 1931 Pan Am opened bids to U.S. aircraft builders. Trippe himself, along with his advisers Preister and Lindbergh, set the requirements for speed, **range**, and payload capacity. Igor Sikorsky, the famous Russian-born pioneer in aircraft design, took up the challenge. Three years later, in 1934, Sikorsky delivered the S-42.

The S-42 was not just a seaplane. It was a flying hotel. For four months Captain Musick ran it through test after test. During this period Musick and the S-42 set ten world records for speed, altitude, and cargo capacity.

Aided by its two pontoon water skis, the S-42 could land smoothly and safely on any kind of water, rough or calm. Its hull was made of duralumin—a light, tough mix of aluminum, copper, and other metals. When it landed, the plane touched down with a few light thumps. Then it slipped through the waves like a warm knife through butter. Musick claimed that the S-42 could land on grass, if necessary, with no harm to passengers.

When fueled to the limit, the S-42 could carry an 8-ton payload a distance of 1,200 miles. This was the furthest any large cargo plane of that time could travel without refueling. But the distance from California to Hawaii was over 2,400 miles—double the S-42's best range.

Sikorsky's S-42 could make the trip to Hawaii only if its seats were replaced by extra gas tanks. With no room left for cargo or passengers, the S-42 would be useful only for survey flights. This meant that Pan Am could use the plane to check out and plan future routes and courses. But flying passengers or cargo for 12 to 18 hours was out of the question—so far.

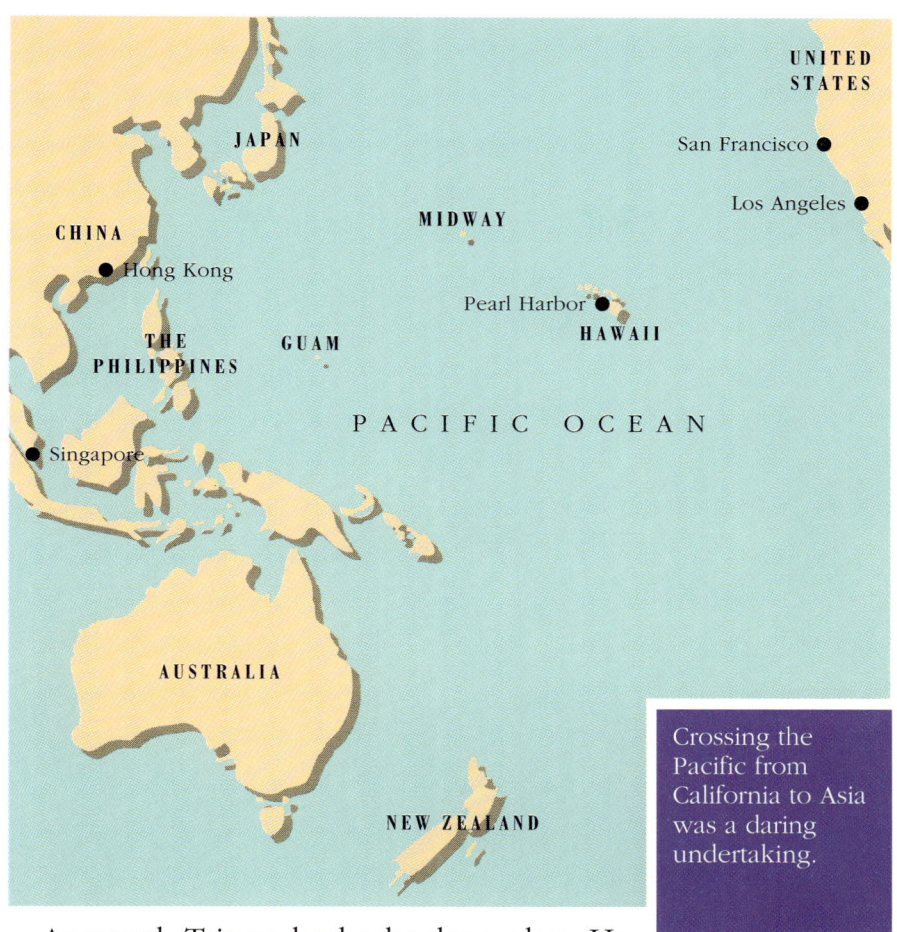

Crossing the Pacific from California to Asia was a daring undertaking.

As usual, Trippe had a backup plan. He had also made a deal with the Maryland plane builder Glenn Luther Martin. In 1932 Martin had begun working on a plane that would be even bigger than the S-42. Two years later, Martin delivered Trippe's flying boat, the M-130. It was flown to California in hops — from Maryland, south to Miami; then down to Acapulco, Mexico; then up to San Diego; and finally north to San Francisco.

Trippe named the M-130 the *China Clipper* in honor of the swift square-rigged clipper ships that had sailed

Hours of hand labor went into building the *China Clipper*.

the seas in the 1800s. The last two digits of the first *China Clipper*'s identification number, NC14716, earned it the affectionate nickname Sweet Sixteen.

Martin's plane was a masterpiece. Ninety-one feet in length, the *China Clipper* was nearly a third longer than the S-42. Its four Pratt and Whitney engines produced over 30 percent more power. They could push the plane through headwinds blowing 50 miles per hour.

Unlike other seaplanes, the M-130 did not land on pontoon skis. The designers believed that skis would cause too much drag, or resistance, during flight. Instead, the new plane had *sponsons*— stubby wings 33 feet wide. They extended from the lower midsection of the plane and made the clipper more stable in the water. These short wings also helped lift the M-130 on takeoff. As a bonus, they stored 950 extra gallons of fuel.

Fully fueled, the M-130 could cut through ocean waves at 60 miles per hour and lift off in 45 seconds. In flight, its cruising speed averaged between 130 and 180 miles per hour.

If necessary, the clipper could stay in flight for nearly 24 hours, something that Musick proved rather unexpectedly. During one test run, he was forced to keep the M-130 in the air for a full 23 hours, 41 minutes. When he finally landed, the fuel tanks were nearly empty. It was good to know just how long the M-130 could actually stay in the air. But still

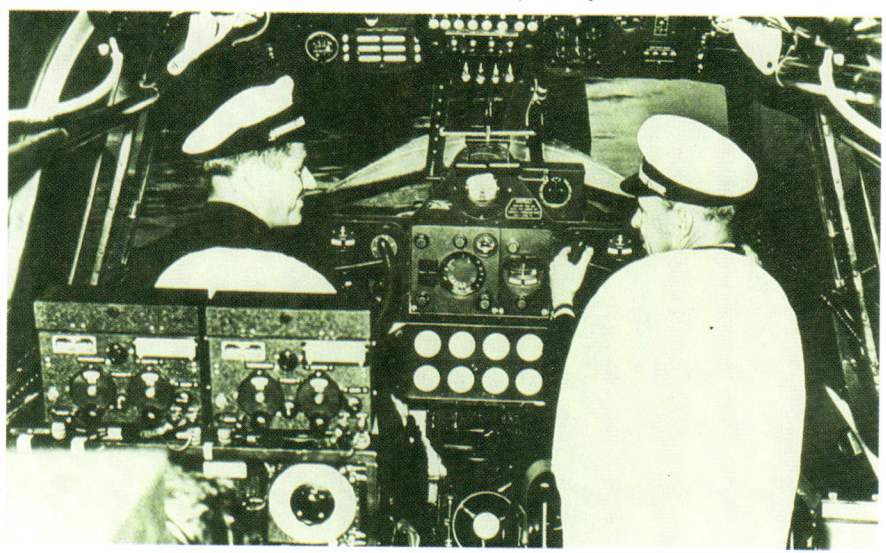

The cockpit was crowded with instruments and controls.

Pan Am wanted to keep up the public's confidence in the plane, so news of this close call never appeared in the press.

The **corrugated**-steel fuselage, or body, of the M-130 was tough and strong. Its lower portion was made of six watertight compartments. Any two of them could keep the plane afloat if the others burst on landing. A second layer of steel strengthened the hull. The plane was even designed so that simple but life-or-death repairs, such as fixing an oil leak, could be made in flight.

The M-130 was as remarkable inside as outside. The interior was divided into three levels. Up front, on the middle deck, was the cockpit. Directly aft, or behind the captain and the first officer, sat the radio officer. Radio equipment picked up weather information from ships and ground stations. Behind the radio officer, upstairs, was the flight engineer's deck.

The flight engineer kept an eye on more than 175 dials and levers. The engineer regulated propeller speeds, engine temperatures, and fuel mixture. A small forward cabin housed the navigation officer, along with maps, compasses, and **chronometers**.

Below the engineer's station was a well-equipped galley, or kitchen, for fixing meals. Next to the galley was bunk space, where two or three crew members at a time could rest on overnight flights. The central cabin, which followed,

The *China Clipper* was like a flying hotel.

could carry cargo or seat up to 12 passengers. It changed into a dining room for meals and, at night, into dressing rooms and sleeping quarters for 8. Eight more people could sleep in two smaller cabins to the rear of the plane.

The tail of the aircraft held enough rafts and emergency supplies to keep people alive for up to three months. Such a disaster, however, seemed unlikely in the solid beauty of the M-130.

In spite of its size, range, and wonderful design, however, the name *China Clipper* said more about Juan Trippe's dreams than about the reality of aviation. At the time, China was still beyond Trippe's reach.

ISLAND BASES

By the mid-1930s, the U.S. Navy had outposts at Pearl Harbor, Guam, and Manila. A plane could land at any of them. But the *China Clipper* could not span the distance between Pearl Harbor and Guam without refueling. Passengers and crew members, too, needed places to rest during overnight layovers.

On a map of the Pacific Ocean, Trippe spotted two small dots, Midway and Wake. Both islands were in the right places, and both were controlled by the U.S. Pan Am had only to turn each into an aviation paradise.

Building airports was not a new challenge for Pan Am. In South America, engineers and building crews had marched through the jungles of Brazil and high into the Andes. They had set up weather stations, radio towers, landing strips, and beacons.

An airport oasis would not appear by magic, however. In the case of sandy Midway and Wake, it meant starting from scratch. So Pan Am chartered the *North Haven,* a 15,000-ton steamer, to deliver 6,000 tons of cargo to the islands. Everything, from topsoil to drinking water, had to be shipped in.

On March 27, 1935, the *North Haven* steamed out of San Francisco with 118 construction workers and technicians. Its cargo included windmills, tractors, furniture, cases of foot powder, combs, and chewing gum. At Honolulu, the *North Haven* took on a ton of dynamite.

Pan Am built grand hotels on Midway and Wake islands.

The water surrounding Midway Island was deep enough for a flying boat to land. But it was too shallow for a steamer to dock. So the *North Haven* had to drop anchor 4 miles away. Equipment and supplies were brought to shore by **barge**. Rough tides and **coral reefs** didn't make delivery easy.

Once on shore, workers dragged supplies over sandbars by tractor. Everywhere were the nests of thousands of gooneys, the large seabirds that inhabited the island. These nests added to the heavy, dangerous work. It took 15 days to

At the hotels on Midway and Wake, *China Clipper* passengers rested in comfort and luxury.

unload just half the cargo. At Wake Island, it was even harder: Workers had to bridge a lagoon with a makeshift railroad.

During construction, work crews lived in tents. Creating airports — even airports for planes that would land at sea — was hot, exhausting work. Nevertheless, airports slowly took shape. On each island, an office was built, followed by storage rooms, a seaplane ramp, a radio station, and living quarters for staff. On Midway, workers even built a nine-hole golf course and a baseball field.

A staff would be needed on each island to service three flights a week. The staff would include a base manager, a radio operator, mechanics, laborers, cooks, and stewards. So some workers would not be returning to the United States for a long while. Instead, they would begin a new life as colonists on a lonely reef.

The first clipper landings with a crew aboard took place in late 1935. But there was still more to do to get the islands ready for the passengers who would stop over on their way across the Pacific. In mid-January 1936, the *North Haven* returned to the islands with another huge delivery. This shipment included two 45-room hotels! Both arrived by boat, ready to assemble. They were identical in every way.

Within 19 months, Midway and Wake each had a hotel open for business. Hotel rooms and services were simple compared with the *China Clipper*'s first-class service. But they still offered all the comforts of home — and more. Every room had a telephone and a private bath, which used solar-heated rainwater or water brought by ship.

Rooms were one thing. But food was a problem all its own. The poor soil on Wake Island did not support a garden. A few fresh vegetables could be grown in water instead of soil. But all other foods had to be brought in by air.

With new hotels and good food, passengers could look forward to comfortable stops at Midway and Wake. Travelers on the clipper could also take comfort in knowing that their planes got top-quality service. While passengers slept through the night in their island hotels, technicians checked every detail of the aircraft, from fuel and oil to electrical wiring. And at each stop, the technicians examined the wing struts for damage and made any needed repairs. Nothing about the plane's — or the passengers' — safety was overlooked.

"AN UNEVENTFUL TRIP"

The *China Clipper*'s first flight from San Francisco to Manila, in the Philippines, came in November 1935. It captured the world's attention. For publicity's sake, Trippe wanted Charles Lindbergh to pilot the flight. Lindbergh, however, had other commitments. So the honor fell to Edwin Musick, who was known for his courage, skill, and coolness under stress.

In his younger days, Musick had thrilled crowds at airshows with his daredevil imitation **dogfights**. Then one imitation battle got a little too real, and Musick's plane went down in flames. Amazingly, both he and his passion for flying survived. But his flying style changed.

After the crash, Musick's bold spirit of adventure was matched by a new concern for detail and form. Again and again, the press wrote about Musick's fussiness over his plane.

Musick had equally high standards for his crew. The six people making the clipper's first, showcase flight

Dressy white uniforms gave the *China Clipper*'s crew a polished, confident look.

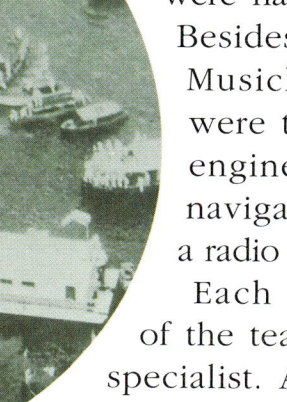

Boats surrounded the clipper soon after it landed.

were handpicked. Besides Captain Musick, there were two flight engineers, two navigators, and a radio operator.

Each member of the team was a specialist. And each was expected to know how to perform at least one other flight job. On a long trip, for example, a flight engineer might take over for the radio operator — or even the pilot — if either one needed rest.

Pan Am required more from its workers than just professional skills. In the 1930s, public trust was the key to growth in aviation. Trippe believed that people would trust a crew more if it looked just right. So Pan Am workers were expected to present a clean-cut, confident image at all times.

Victor Wright, a flight engineer on the *China Clipper*'s first flight to Manila, recalled how busy the crew was. Right after takeoff, the crew changed from uniforms to comfortable clothes. Wright spent the 21-hour flight from San Francisco to Pearl Harbor in red pajamas and slippers. But he never slept. Instead, he "walked to Hawaii," running from one end of the plane to the other. He checked on fuel flow, wind drift, and engine performance.

Shortly before landing in Hawaii, the crew shaved and changed back into uniform. Although they were exhausted when they landed, crew members looked fresh and bright. From the crew's relaxed appearance, onlookers would think that the 21-hour flight had been as refreshing and ordinary as a brisk autumn walk. That was exactly the image Pan Am wanted to create in order to sell people on air travel.

The transpacific flight made Musick an instant American hero. His picture was in the news and on the cover of *Time* magazine. Fame, however, was a bother for Musick. He was a man of few words, someone who did not enjoy publicity one bit. But wherever he went, reporters followed, and photographers popped up at every turn.

Passengers and crew members always received a big greeting.

On arriving in Hawaii, he was surrounded by reporters begging for an interview. In answer to questions about the history-making flight, Musick made a five-word speech: "Without incident, an uneventful trip."

CHAPTER 6

FLYING TO CHINA

On October 21, 1936, the first commercial flight to Manila left from Alameda, California. More than 1,000 people applied to be among the first seven passengers. Round-trip fare was $1,600—the price of a comfortable house during the 1930s.

The final passenger list read like a society-page "who's who." Included were a San Francisco **industrialist**, a chain-store executive, the owner of a string of grocery stores, and a manager from Standard Oil. Two women passengers were identified as "world travelers." Like the others, they rode in quiet elegance, insulated from the roar of engines, changes in temperature, and the cares of the world.

The *China Clipper* set new standards for air travel. In the best planes owned by other airlines, passengers had to shout to be heard over the engines' howl. At higher altitudes they shivered from cold. In the *China Clipper*'s soundproofed cabins, people could talk in normal tones. An air-conditioning and heating system kept temperatures comfortable at all times.

Beautiful colors, fashionable **Art Deco** design, and soft dome lights pleased the eye. Venetian blinds at the larger windows provided shade from harsh sunlight. Thick carpets and deep upholstery added to a feeling of safety, luxury, and romance.

The clipper had plenty of room for games and relaxation.

Dinner on the clipper was formal — and delicious.

Stewards stood ready like genies. Their job was to grant passengers their every wish, from morning cups of hot chocolate in bed to nighttime "tuck-ins."

One of Trippe's major goals was to get the public to believe in air travel. This first flight was supposed to show that flying was romantic but routine, adventurous but safe. Every detail of the flight was geared to achieve that aim. Fortunately for Trippe, his plan succeeded.

Soon clipper fever swept the nation. Clippers were pictured on postage stamps. Across the United States, hundreds of restaurants were named the China Clipper.

A dance called the China Clipper became popular. Even Hollywood celebrated the fabulous flying boat. The 1936 film *China Clipper* starred the box-office idol Humphrey Bogart.

By late spring 1937, clipper service reached all the way to China. Weekly flights to Macau and Hong Kong also were in full swing.

The transpacific flights were stlll trying to compete with the great ocean liners. And even though travel time was reduced from several weeks by sea to less than a week by air, the trip was as luxurious as a cruise.

Meals on the *China Clipper* were not like today's heat-and-eat airplane food. A typical clipper menu offered roast prime rib, veal cutlets, chicken fricassee, lobster, avocado salad, asparagus, champagne, pineapple pie, and chocolate sundaes. Everything was served on tables set with linen, silver, crystal, and white china bearing the blue Pan Am logo.

Between meals, people could sit in living-room comfort, sipping coffee, tea, or cocoa and eating fancy cakes. They could even snack on fresh strawberries in cream.

While passengers dined or relaxed, the steward turned their cabin seats into beds. Upper and lower bunks were created, and a stepladder led to the top. The bunks were draped with snap-on curtains for privacy.

Flying west to Asia, the clippers crossed the international dateline between Midway and Wake. To celebrate losing a day, passengers received gold-lettered certificates. Sometimes, at night, entertainment was provided by an ocean liner. The radio operator would send a message down to ask that the ship let all its lights blaze. Then the pilot of the clipper would swoop down so passengers could enjoy the brilliant show of lights.

The 56 hours in the air were divided by island layovers. To keep the landing area smooth and safe, boats cleared away any floating junk. When a clipper touched down, the wing flaps helped guide it through the water. Passengers stepped off the plane into small boats, or launches, which took them to shore.

Passengers enjoyed comfortable bunks and sofas.

The clipper's crew welcomed passengers aboard.

Upon arriving in Hawaii, passengers were greeted with ginger blossom leis, or wreaths of flowers. Midway and Wake also came to life when guests arrived. Here, waiting station wagons drove passengers to their hotels. Fresh flowers filled every room.

On the Midway layover, passengers could play baseball, tennis, or golf. They could also go fish-gazing in glass-bottom boats. Of course, anywhere on Midway gooneys were on hand to entertain or pose for pictures.

When a clipper left from Hawaii, coconut milk was poured over the bow for good luck. Very little was left to luck, however. Pilots had to pass four levels of training: apprentice, junior, senior, and captain. Most of the pilots, flight engineers, navigators, and radio experts were trained in the U.S. Navy. Before the pilots could become captains, they had to log 2,000 hours of flight time. Clipper travel was designed to be as safe as it was elegant.

CHAPTER 7

THE END OF AN ERA

While Pan Am expanded into the Pacific, the Japanese government watched with increasing displeasure. Japan viewed Pan Am's growth as another sign of American aggression. As far back as 1935, Japan had tried to keep Pan Am away from the Pacific. FBI agents had even caught Japanese spies tampering with the *China Clipper*'s direction finder. It seemed clear the spies' goal was to **sabotage** the first mail run to Manila!

By 1938, Japan was making claims on much of the Pacific. The stage was set for war.

Japan's minister of foreign affairs warned the United States to stop the clipper flights to Macau and Hong Kong. Pan Am ignored the warning. Shortly after, whether by coincidence or not, the *Hawaii Clipper* disappeared between Guam and Macau, never to be found. Although there are many theories, no one really knows what happened.

Passengers lined up to meet the famous Sweet Sixteen.

Taking the loss in stride, Trippe allowed his vision to grow. Much of the globe didn't have air service yet, and Trippe wasted no time going for it. In 1939 he added an even bigger, more luxurious plane to Pan Am's clipper fleet — the B-314. Built by Boeing Aircraft, the plane even had a honeymoon suite.

In 1940 the B-314 *California Clipper* started regular service from Los Angeles to New Zealand. Shortly before, a tragedy had occurred along this same route. On a 1938 survey flight along the Los Angeles-to-New Zealand route, Captain Musick had lost his life. An oil leak caused his Sikorsky plane, the *Samoa Clipper*, to explode while it

The sight of two clippers together was unusual.

was over the ocean. All that remained were fragments. No trace of Musick or any of his crew was ever found.

All the while, tension between Japan and the United States increased. The conflict finally exploded into war on December 7, 1941, when Japan bombed the U.S. Navy base at Pearl Harbor, Hawaii. The United States and Japan went to war.

Pan Am's clipper route — and several of the clippers themselves — also suffered serious damage in Japanese attacks. On the very same day that Pearl Harbor was attacked, the *Philippine Clipper*, resting at Wake Island, was splattered with 60 bullets. The damaged plane unloaded its cargo and managed to get Pan Am workers and passengers safely to Midway. It was a scary ride indeed. The bullets had destroyed the plane's direction finder. So Pan Am workers on Midway built huge fires to guide the rescue flight to a safe landing.

The *Hong Kong Clipper*, a Sikorsky S-42, was about to leave Hong Kong for Manila. On December 8, the day after Pearl Harbor, Japanese bombers destroyed it. Meanwhile, the U.S. bombed the Macau airfield to keep American planes out of enemy hands. Guam and Manila also fell to the Japanese.

As soon as war broke out, Pan Am handed over ten clippers to the U.S. Navy. Eight of the planes entered military service in the Atlantic. They assisted American forces in Europe. The history-making *China Clipper* and the battle-scarred *Philippine Clipper* stayed in the Pacific. They shuttled military people and medical supplies back and forth between San Francisco and Honolulu.

Today, however, none of the original transpacific clipper fleet remains. The *Philippine Clipper* crashed on a mountain near Ukiah, California, in January 1943. All 19 people aboard were killed. Just two years later, the *China Clipper* struck a submerged object in the waters off Trinidad, in the Caribbean. Only 7 of its 30 passengers survived.

Between flights, crews checked the planes thoroughly.

As World War II raged on, the enormous flying boats became less and less practical. On April 8, 1946, the *American Clipper*—a Boeing B-314—went out of service after a Honolulu–San Francisco flight. The surviving clippers were scrapped or sold to collectors. The era of elegant clippers winging across the Pacific had come to a close.

Other Pan Am planes, however, continued to circle the globe for nearly five more decades. But in 1970 Pan Am's fortunes took an unexpected nosedive. The airline was deeply in debt from purchasing new planes. Then it ran into another problem. During the 1970s, fuel became so scarce and so expensive that, during one week in 1973, the cost of aviation gas increased 400 percent.

In the past, the government had helped Pan Am. One reason was that Pan Am had expanded airmail service for the United States Post Office. Another reason was that Pan Am had set up air bases in the Pacific that the U.S. military needed to use. But in the 1970s, new laws prevented the government from saving the airline.

Pan Am held on all through the 1980s. To keep itself alive, the struggling airline sold whatever it could—planes, its skyscraper headquarters in New York, an international chain of hotels, and even its transatlantic routes. But, on December 4, 1991, after 64 years of flight, the fabulous clipper airline was grounded for good. Everything was sold, everything, that is, but what could never be bought or forgotten—a legacy of adventure and romance done with a great deal of class.

In the air, the *China Clipper* was all grace and power.

GLOSSARY

Art Deco ✈ A style of decoration popular in the early 20th century, featuring geometric shapes and bold colors.
barge ✈ A flat-bottomed boat used to carry freight.
chronometer ✈ A very accurate clock, used in science and navigation.
clipper ship ✈ A large sailing ship of the 19th century, built for speed with a narrow width and many sails.
commercial aviation ✈ Flying aircraft as a business.
coral reef ✈ A narrow ridge near the surface of the water made of coral, a hard, stony substance formed by the skeletons of many tiny sea animals.
corrugated ✈ Having a wavy surface, with ridges and hollows.
dogfight ✈ A battle between airplanes.
Great Depression ✈ A worldwide business slump during the 1930s; it left millions of people unemployed and in poverty.
industrialist ✈ A person who owns or manages an industry.
range ✈ The distance a vehicle can travel on one supply of fuel.
sabotage ✈ The destruction of a country's factories, transportation, etc., by enemy agents.
transpacific ✈ Across the Pacific Ocean.

FURTHER READING

Ayers, Carter M. *Pilots and Aviation.* Minneapolis: Lerner Publications, 1990.

Berliner, Don. *Distance Flights.* Minneapolis: Lerner Publications, 1990.

Burleigh, Robert. *Flight.* New York: Philomel Books, 1991.

Emert, Phyllis. *Helicopters.* New York: Julian Messner, 1990.

Gunning, Thomas. *Dream Trains.* New York: Dillon Press, 1992.

Lindbloom, Steven. *Fly the Hot Ones.* Boston: Houghton Mifflin, 1991.

Munro, Roxie. *Blimps.* New York: E.P. Dutton, 1989.

INDEX

American Clipper, 43
Atlantic Ocean, 14, 42
B-314, 40, 43
Boeing Aircraft, 40
California Clipper, 40
Caribbean Sea, 14, 42
Central America, 14
China, 23, 35
China Clipper, 5, 6, 7, 9, 10, 19, 20, 23, 24, 27, 28, 30, 32, 34, 35, 39, 42
Colonial Air Transport, 12
Europe, 16, 42
FBI (Federal Bureau of Investigation), 39
Guam, 7, 24, 39, 42
Havana, Cuba, 12, 14
Hawaii, 7, 18, 30, 31, 37
Hawaii Clipper, 39
Hong Kong, 35, 39, 42
Hong Kong Clipper, 42
Honolulu, Hawaii, 7, 9, 17, 25, 42
Japan, 39, 41
Key West, Florida, 12, 14
Lindbergh, Charles, 14, 17, 28
Luzon, Philippines, 7
M-130, 19, 20, 21, 22, 23
Macau, 35, 39, 42
Manila, Philippines, 7, 9, 24, 28, 30, 32, 39, 42
Martin, Glenn Luther, 19, 20
Midway, 7, 24, 25, 26, 27, 35, 37, 42
Musick, Captain Edwin, 7, 14, 28, 30, 31, 40, 41

Navy Flying Corps, 11
Newfoundland, 15
New York, New York, 12, 44
North Haven, 25, 27
Pacific Ocean, 7, 16, 24, 27, 39, 42, 43, 44
Pan American Airways, 10, 12, 14, 15, 17, 18, 24, 25, 30, 35, 39, 40, 41, 42, 44
Pearl Harbor, 17, 24, 30, 41, 42
Philippine Clipper, 41, 42
Philippines, 7, 9, 28
Pratt and Whitney, 6, 20
Preister, André, 14, 17
Roosevelt, Franklin Delano, 7
S-42, 18, 19, 20, 42
Samoa Clipper, 40
San Diego, California, 19
San Francisco, California, 7, 9, 17, 19, 25, 28, 30, 32, 42, 43
Sikorsky, Igor, 17, 18, 40
South America, 14, 24
Trippe, Juan, 7, 10, 11, 12, 14, 15, 16, 17, 19, 23, 24, 28, 30, 34, 40
United States (U.S.), 15, 24, 26, 34, 39, 41, 42
U.S. Navy, 24, 37, 41, 42
United States Post Office, 44
Wake, 7, 24, 26, 27, 35, 37, 41
World War I, 14
World War II, 43

CODMAN SQUARE

WITHDRAWN
No longer the property of the
Boston Public Library.
Sale of this material benefits the Library.